So...
You Want the Law of Attraction to Work

LINDA MITTS

Brilliant Books Literary
137 Forest Park Lane Thomasville
North Carolina 27360 USA

Acknowledgement

I would like to acknowledge and thank my husband, Dwight, for all the support, belief in me, and his dedication to helping me achieve my dream.

I would also like to acknowledge and thank Marilyn for her encouragement and technical support. She was my turn-to-gal.

INTRODUCTION

The Law of Attraction has been around forever. After all, it is a Law of the Universe – much like the Law of Gravity. Whether or not you believe it, the Law of Attraction is at work in your life.

The movie _The Secret,_ that debuted in 2006, finally made the Law better known and easier to understand. Since that time, millions of books have been published to help people understand the Law of Attraction and to facilitate the Law working for them.

I have been one of those people investing in books and programs. I have gone to live events, trying to find a way to get the Law of Attraction to work for me. Many times I felt so close, only to have it "disappear" again. I discovered that I was not alone.

My passion is to help as many people as I can during my lifetime, in ways that significantly improve their lives. For 38 years this passion was met by teaching special education K-12. During those 38 years, I discovered that there is not just one way to teach. Teaching involves many different approaches and materials to facilitate learning, and more importantly understand the concepts. I do not feel another book or program is the answer. "Teaching", using many different concepts already in existence, is a unique and more appropriate way, to me.

I have created this "Course" to expose a person to valuable materials specifically related to the Law of Attraction. Each lesson comes with guidance to accomplish that lesson. It is my goal to help you understand the material at a deeper level.

The materials I chose were based upon: being easy to read and understand; using a variety of formats; and reasonably priced or free.

Welcome and enjoy your Journey!

CONTENTS

LESSON 1 — THE SECRET

Watch the movie *The Secret*. You can watch it for free at https://www.youtube.com/watch?v=GW2I6-Ig49A.

This movie brought to light the Law of Attraction. There is more to the Law than you see in the movie. However, it is an excellent beginning.

The movie is divided up into 10 sections. The first section explains the history of the "Secret". Most notable in this section is the fact that the "Secret" was coveted and hidden away.

The second section discusses how feelings are used to guide you in using the "Secret". It talks about what the high vibrations are, as well as the low vibrations, and the consequences of being "in that mood". It is easy to switch out of being in a low state by having "Secret Shifters". Bob Proctor gives you some suggestions.

In the third section demonstrates how to use the "Secret". Please note suggestions made in this section that explains what to do when you feel stuck.

The last sections are specific to subjects like Money, Relationships, Health, the World, You, and Life. There are key components in each of these to pay attention to.

As you watch the movie, **pay special attention** to the presenters, their ideas and quotes. Have a pen and paper next to you while watching. If you have already seen the movie, please watch it again and look deeper for things you might have missed the first time. Each time I have watched it, something new pops out. That is because I am coming from a different point than I had previously.

Pick ten (10) presenters and explain three (3) different ideas they expressed in the movie. Explain what their ideas mean to you.

Presenter 1:

Idea 1 ~ _____

_____

_____

_____

_____

Idea 2 ~ _____

_____

_____

_____

_____

Idea 3 ~ _____

_____

_____

_____

_____

Presenter 2:

Idea 1 ~ _____

_____

_____

_____

_____

Idea 2 ~ _____

_____

_____

_____

_____

Idea 3 ~ _____

_____

_____

_____

_____

Presenter 3: _____

Idea 1 ~ _____

_____

_____

_____

_____

Idea 2 ~ _____

_____

_____

_____

_____

Idea 3 ~ _____

_____

_____

_____

_____

Presenter 4:

Idea 1 ~ _____

_____

_____

_____

_____

Idea 2 ~ _____

_____

_____

_____

_____

Idea 3 ~ _____

_____

_____

_____

_____

Presenter 5:

Idea 1 ~ _____

_____

_____

_____

_____

Idea 2 ~ _____

_____

_____

_____

_____

Idea 3 ~ _____

_____

_____

_____

_____

Presenter 6:

Idea 1 ~ _____

_____

_____

_____

_____

Idea 2 ~ _____

_____

_____

_____

_____

Idea 3 ~ _____

_____

_____

_____

_____

Presenter 7:

Idea 1 ~ _____

_____

_____

_____

_____

Idea 2 ~ _____

_____

_____

_____

_____

Idea 3 ~ _____

_____

_____

_____

_____

Presenter 8:

Idea 1 ~ _____
_____
_____
_____
_____

Idea 2 ~ _____
_____
_____
_____
_____

Idea 3 ~ _____
_____
_____
_____
_____

Presenter 9:

Idea 1 ~ _____
_____
_____
_____
_____

Idea 2 ~ _____
_____
_____
_____
_____

Idea 3 ~ _____

_____
_____
_____
_____

Presenter 10:

Idea 1 ~ _____

_____
_____
_____
_____

Idea 2 ~ _____

_____
_____
_____
_____

Idea 3 ~ _____

_____
_____
_____
_____

List five (5) quotes that were presented in the movie and explain what each of them mean to you.

Quote 1: _____

_____

_____

_____

_____

Quote 2: _____

_____

_____

_____

_____

Quote 3: _____

_____

_____

_____

_____

Quote 4: _____

_____

_____

_____

_____

Quote 5: _____

_____

_____

_____

_____

<u>OVERVIEW</u>

Write your impression of the movie as a whole:

What did you learn? _____

_____

_____

_____

_____

What caught your attention? _____

_____

_____

_____

_____

What seemed foolish or laughable? _____

_____

_____

_____

_____

Do you feel the Law of Attraction will work for you? Why or why not? _____

_____

_____

_____

_____

_____

_____

_____

_____

LESSON 2 — E-CUBED

Purchase, borrow or check out the book *E-Cubed* by Pam Grout. In this book there are nine (9) do-it-yourself energy experiments that prove **your thoughts create your reality.**

Pam uses a "scientific method" as her format for each of the experiments. She utilizes this to keep the results "factual" versus "opinion". I find that her set up for the experiments is unique, but it allows one to come to definite conclusions.

It is important to keep an open mind when doing the experiments. It works better if you try not to prejudge the results you think you might get. Above all, follow the experiments as if you were on a mission to get the results. These experiments are fun to do, so please enjoy.

These experiments may take several days, as many of the experiments cannot be accomplished in one day. Therefore, do something in this book every day until you are finished.

Use the following space to document your results. This way the entire course results will be available in one place.

Experiment #1: THE BOOGIE-WOOGIE COROLLARY

Results: _____
_____
_____
_____
_____

Implications for you: _____
_____
_____
_____
_____

Experiment #2: THE RED PILL COROLLARY

Results: _____
_____
_____
_____
_____

Implications for you: _____
_____
_____
_____
_____

Experiment #3: THE SIMON COWELL COROLLARY

Results: _____

_____

_____

_____

_____

Implications for you: _____

_____

_____

_____

_____

Experiment #4: "I'M LOVING AND I KNOW IT" COROLLARY

Results: _____

_____

_____

_____

_____

Implications for you: _____

_____

_____

_____

_____

Experiment #5   YOUR NEW B.F.F. COROLLARY

Results: _____

_____

_____

_____

_____

Implications for you: _____

_____

_____

_____

_____

Experiment #6: THE NATURE VS. NEWS COROLLARY

Results: _____

_____

_____

_____

_____

Implications for you: _____

_____

_____

_____

_____

Experiment #7: THE "IF YOU SAY SO" COROLLARY

Results: _____

_____

_____

_____

_____

Implications for you: _____

_____

_____

_____

_____

Experiment #8   THE PLACEBO COROLLARY

Results: _____

_____

_____

_____

_____

Implications for you: _____

_____

_____

_____

_____

Experiment #9   THE YABBA-DABBA-DOO COROLLARY

Results: _____

_____

_____

_____

_____

Implications for you: _____

_____

_____

_____

_____

OVERVIEW

Describe your thoughts, your feelings, and the facts you obtained from reading the book and performing the exercises:

_____

_____

_____

_____

_____

_____

_____

_____

_____

_____

_____

_____

_____

_____

_____

_____

_____

_____

What correlation(s) did you find, if any, to <u>The Secret</u>?

_____

_____

_____

_____

_____

_____

_____

_____

_____

_____

_____

LESSON 3—THE SCIENCE OF GETTING RICH

The next assignment is to read <u>The Science of Getting Rich</u> by Wallace D. Wattles. This book was written and published in 1910. You can get the book free at http://ebooksoneverything.com/wealth/scienceofgettingrich.pdf

It is stated in the preface, that this book is written for people who want to get rich. Therefore, it is written in such a way as to guide you by telling you what you need to do.

In chapter 1, what is his philosophy about being rich?

_____

_____

_____

_____

In chapter 2, he states "It is a natural law that like causes always produce like effect; and, therefore any man or woman who learns to do things in this certain way will infallibly get rich." What is one fact that he uses to prove this? _____

_____

_____

_____

_____

In chapter 3, how does he define "Formless Stuff"? What would you call it today? _____

_____

_____

_____

_____

In chapter 4, what are the three (3) fundamental propositions? _____

_____

_____

_____

_____

In chapter 5, what are 3 reasons he gives for being rich?

_____

_____

_____

_____

In chapter 6, what is the one thing that Wattles believes you must give every man? _____

_____

_____

_____

_____

In chapter 7, what is so important about gratitude?

_____

_____

_____

In chapter 8, what are the three (3) steps to getting rich?

_____

_____

_____

_____

In chapter 9, what are you NOT to do? _____

_____

_____

_____

_____

In chapter 10, what are you to stay away from? _____

_____

_____

_____

_____

In chapter 11, what are you to do beyond thinking, and why? _____

_____

_____

_____

_____

In chapter 12, what is the biggest wrong you can do? ____

_____

_____

_____

_____

In chapter 13, what is meant by getting into the right business? _____

_____

_____

_____

_____

In chapter 14, what is meant by increase? _____

_____

_____

_____

_____

In chapter 15, who is the man that is certain to advance?

_____

_____

_____

_____

In chapter 16, what are two (2) factors that can "betray" your creative plane? _____

_____

_____

_____

_____

In chapter 17, what are three (3) elements that stand out the most to you? _____

_____

_____

_____

_____

OVERVIEW

What were at least five "take aways" from this book. In other words, what did you learn? _____

_____

_____

_____

_____

_____

_____

****

What similarities did you find between <u>The Secret</u> and <u>The Science of Getting Rich?</u> _____

_____

_____

_____

_____

What were some differences? _____

_____

_____

_____

_____

What concepts, if any, did it clarify for you? _____

_____

_____

_____

_____

What, if any, new concepts were presented? _____

_____

_____

_____

_____

LESSON 4—ATTRACT MONEY NOW

The next book I want you to read is <u>Attract Money Now</u> by Dr. Joe Vitale. This book can be obtained free at <u>www.attractmoneynow.com</u>. You do NOT need Adobe Flash. You will receive a link to the book via email. You do NOT need to complete the Miracles Coaching Questionnaire to receive the link.

In this book, Dr. Vitale gives you a seven-step process, or blueprint, for attracting money. For each of the steps, he explains why that step is important. He offers practical strategies to help you better understand.

What are 3 bullets in the "Grasping the Golden Ring – Truths and Take Aways" that have the most meaning for you? _____

_____

_____

_____

_____

_____

Write your answers to the Action Steps. _____

_____
_____
_____
_____
_____
_____
_____
_____
_____

Step 1 – Alter How You Think

Which of the three limiting beliefs that Joe talks about, do you feel is the strongest for you/why? _____

_____
_____
_____
_____

How does Joe suggest releasing them? _____

_____
_____
_____
_____

What are 3 bullets in Step 1 that were the most meaningful for you? _____

_____
_____
_____
_____

Write your answers to the Action Steps. _____

_____
_____
_____
_____
_____
_____

Step 2 – Give Without Expectation

What are the two levels of giving? _____

_____
_____
_____

What are 3 bullets in Step 2 that were the most meaningful for you? _____

_____
_____
_____

Write your answers to the Action Steps. _____

_____
_____
_____

Step 3 – Prosperous Spending

Give an example of what this quote means to you "Rewards don't have to involve large amounts of money – but they should generate large amounts of positive feelings and emotion." _____

_____

_____

_____

_____

Joe talked about going to a mall to listen to people's conversations, to hear how many negative and positive statements they make. I would encourage you to do that and record your observations. _____

_____

_____

_____

_____

What are 3 bullets in Step 3 that were the most meaningful for you? _____

_____

_____

_____

_____

Write your answers to the Action Steps. _____

_____

_____

_____

_____

Step 4 – Ask For Help

What two things does asking for help accomplish? _____

What are the two (2) levels of asking? _____

What are some advantages to having a Mastermind Group? _____

What did you find meaningful in the section *The Kindness of Strangers*? _____

What are 3 bullets in Step 4 that were the most meaningful for you? _____

Write your answers to the Action Steps. _____

_____

_____

_____

_____

Step 5 —Nevillize Your Goals

What is the first step in Nevillizing your goal? _____

_____

_____

_____

_____

What is vision mapping? _____

_____

_____

_____

_____

What are the three things needed to increase talent and go toward greatness according to The Talent Code?

_____

_____

_____

_____

What are 3 bullets in Step 5 that were the most meaningful for you? _____

_____

_____

_____

_____

Write your answers to the Action Steps. _____

_____
_____
_____
_____
_____
_____

Step 6 – Think Like An Entrepreneur

Joe talks about evaluating a potential source of income on page 89. What are the important things to keep in mind? _____

_____
_____
_____
_____

What are some suggestions that Joe makes for the internet? _____

_____
_____
_____
_____

What are 3 bullets in Step 6 that were the most meaningful for you? _____

_____
_____
_____
_____

Write your answers to the Action Steps. _____

_____

_____

_____

_____

_____

_____

_____

Step 7 – Help Your Community and Your World

What is the purpose of the "Light Switch" analogy?

_____

_____

_____

_____

What does persistence have to do with attracting money?

_____

_____

_____

_____

What is important about inspiring others? _____

_____

_____

_____

_____

What are 3 bullets in Step 7 that were the most meaningful for you? _____

_____

_____

_____

_____

_____

Write your answers to the Action Steps. _____

_____

_____

_____

_____

_____

The Freedom to Live!

What is important about gratitude? _____

_____

_____

_____

_____

What are somethings in the section *The Power of Now* that you found interesting? _____

_____

_____

_____

_____

_____

So...You Want the Law of Attraction to Work

So...You Want the Law of Attraction to Work

What are somethings in the section *Reaching New Heights* that you found interesting? _____

_____

_____

_____

_____

What are some of the things listed in *29 Ways to Attract Money Now* that you found inspiring? _____

_____

_____

_____

_____

Joe talks about many facets of goals and goal setting in the Super Bonus section *The Secret to Attract Money Now! The How: Setting Effective Goals.* What are the important steps in Setting Effective Goals? Give a brief explanation of each. _____

_____

_____

_____

_____

_____

In the last Bonus section *A Divine Way to Clear Limiting Beliefs About Money*, Joe talks about ho'oponopono. What are the four (4) phrases that are repeated? _____

_____

_____

_____

_____

What are your impressions of ho'oponopono? _____

_____

_____

_____

_____

OVERVIEW

Write a summary of your impression(s) of <u>Attract Money Now.</u>

_____

_____

_____

_____

_____

_____

_____

_____

LESSON 5 – LAW OF ATTRACTION

Check out, borrow or purchase <u>Law of Attraction</u> by Michael Loiser.

On page 6, he explains why his book is different. His approach is more concrete and easy to follow. On page 7, he defines the Law of Attraction. What is his definition?

_____

_____

_____

_____

On page 13, Michael talks about "vibes". What does this have to do with the Law of Attraction? _____

_____

_____

_____

_____

On page 17, explain what non-deliberate attraction is.

_____
_____
_____
_____

On page 21, what does Michael say about words? _____

_____
_____
_____
_____

On page 31, what are the key components to Step 1 – Identify Your Desire. _____

_____
_____
_____
_____

Completing the exercises on pages 41-48 would be beneficial.

Starting on page 51, Step 2 is explained. What are the key components discussed? _____

_____
_____
_____
_____

In step 3, on page 73, there are 9 outstanding tools that he suggests using. I would encourage you to utilize these tools by completing all the exercises.

Which 3 tools did you find most beneficial and why?

_____

_____

_____

_____

_____

_____

The last section is Beyond the 3-step Formula on page 111. This section is worthy of reading because it expands on the key concepts discussed earlier. List 5 things in the last section that helped make the Law of Attraction more concrete. _____

_____

_____

_____

_____

OVERVIEW

What did you like/dislike about his presentation of the Law of Attraction and why? _____

_____

_____

_____

_____

What are the major differences between <u>Law of Attraction</u> and <u>Attract Money Now</u>? _____

_____

_____

_____

_____

Which one do you feel more comfortable applying and why? _____

_____

_____

_____

_____

_____

LESSON 6—THE 11 FORGOTTEN LAWS

The 11 Forgotten Laws is a program designed by Bob Proctor that facilitates the understanding of the Law of Attraction. The Law of Attraction is one of the 11 forgotten laws. It is difficult to understand the 11 Laws if you try to do them all at once. I strongly encourage you to do just one a day. If you are comfortable doing more than one a day, and can fully grasp the concepts, feel free to move forward more quickly. Go to this website to hear Bob Proctor explain each of them:

https://www.youtube.com/watch?v=lQ1TnBtqAg4&list=PL46AACBA4BE7B293D

After listening to each law, write the major concept or concepts you gathered from the material.

Introduction _____

_____

_____

_____

_____

1. Law of Attraction _____

_____

_____

_____

_____

_____

_____

2. Law of Non-Resistance _____

_____

_____

_____

_____

_____

3. Law of Receiving _____

_____

_____

_____

_____

_____

4. Law of Thinking _____

_____

_____

_____

_____

_____

5. Law of Supply _____

_____
_____
_____
_____
_____
_____

6. Law of Sacrifice _____

_____
_____
_____
_____
_____
_____

7. Law of Compensation _____

_____
_____
_____
_____
_____
_____

8. Law of Increase _____

_____
_____
_____
_____
_____
_____

9. Law of Obedience _____

_____

_____

_____

_____

_____

_____

10. Law of Success _____

_____

_____

_____

_____

_____

_____

11. Law of Forgiveness _____

_____

_____

_____

_____

_____

_____

****

OVERVIEW
What is your impression of this assignment? _____

_____

_____

_____

What, if anything, helped you develop a better under-standing?

_____

_____

_____

_____

_____

_____

What is your favorite Law and why? _____

_____

_____

_____

_____

_____

Which Law did you find most confusing and why?_____

_____

_____

_____

_____

_____

What will you do with this information? How will you apply it? _____

_____

_____

_____

_____

_____

I encourage you to participate in the following Optional Assignments. They are well worth the time.

OPTIONAL ASSIGNMENT

LESSON 7—DOWN THE RABBIT HOLE

Watch the DVD movie <u>Down the Rabbit Hole</u>. It is available for purchase, at some libraries, or you may watch it for free online. The YouTube video is in two parts.

PART 1
https://www.youtube.com/
watch?feature=player_detailpage&v=qRHKVArA690

PART 2
https://www.youtube.com/
watch?v=OhnHFnajMB4&feature=player_detailpage

In the event the above links do not work properly, copy the links below into your YouTube search browser.

PART 1
what.the.bleep.down.the.rabbit.hole.2006.dvdrip.xvid.imbt.cd1

PART 2
what.the.bleep.down.the.rabbit.hole.2006.dvdrip.xvid.
imbt.cd2.avi

Down the Rabbit Hole explains quantum physics as it relates to the Law of Attraction, in simple layman terms. It is an in-depth look at how we really do have a say in our lives.

Have a pen and paper available as you watch this movie and log at least 25 notes of areas that had an impact on you. Also, write down any questions that come to mind as you watch the movie.

Pay particular attention to the Section on Waves and Particles, as it provides the best explanation of the Law of Attraction. You will learn that the "Observer" (you) can alter the perception of the outcome. Your energy specifically impacts the universe/spirit energy which we are surrounded by. This is the key to understanding that what we think about, will come about!

As you watch Down the Rabbit Hole, you will find that modern-day Science supports the same philosophies as presented in The Secret and in The Science of Getting Rich. You will see and understand that everything you want in life is possible!

Note 1 ~ _____

_____

_____

_____

_____

Note 2 ~ _____

_____

_____

_____

_____

Note 3 ~ _____

_____

_____

_____

_____

Note 4 ~ _____

_____

_____

_____

_____

Note 5 ~ _____

_____

_____

_____

_____

Note 6 ~ _____

_____

_____

_____

_____

Note 7 ~ _____

_____

_____

_____

_____

Note 8 ~ _____

_____

_____

_____

_____

Note 9 ~ _____

_____

_____

_____

_____

Note 10 ~ _____

_____

_____

_____

_____

Note 11 ~ _____

_____

_____

_____

_____

Note 12 ~ _____

_____

_____

_____

_____

Note 13 ~ _____

_____

_____

_____

_____

Note 14 ~ _____

_____

_____

_____

_____

Note 15 ~ _____

_____

_____

_____

_____

Note 16 ~ _____

_____

_____

_____

_____

Note 17 ~ _____

_____
_____
_____
_____

Note 18 ~ _____

_____
_____
_____
_____

Note 19 ~ _____

_____
_____
_____
_____

Note 20 ~ _____

_____
_____
_____
_____

Note 21 ~ _____

_____
_____
_____
_____

Note 22 ~ _____

_____

_____

_____

_____

Note 23 ~ _____

_____

_____

_____

_____

Note 24 ~ _____

_____

_____

_____

_____

Note 25 ~ _____

_____

_____

_____

_____

OVERVIEW

What was your impression of the movie? _____

_____

_____

_____

_____

How will you use the knowledge conveyed in the movie?

_____

_____

_____

_____

What were some of the "WOW" moments you encountered while watching the movie? _____

_____

_____

_____

_____

What are some questions you still have? _____

_____

_____

_____

_____

OPTIONAL ASSIGNMENT

Lesson 8— The Passion Test

As you have gone through these assignments, one element that has been touched on is ***finding your passion***. It has been documented that finding happiness and abundance is much easier when working on something you are passionate about. Some say your passion is also your purpose on this Earth and if you follow your passion, money and happiness will come. There are many different processes to help you find your passion, however, the easiest one I found is <u>The Passion Test</u>. You can get a free passion test at http://www.thepassiontest.com. Click START on the left as soon as page pops up. It is a simple test and will be very useful in helping you identify your true life passion.

What were your results? Your passion(s)? _____

_____

_____

_____

_____

_____

What clarity did this provide you? _____

_____

_____

_____

_____

_____

_____

_____

_____

_____

Are you in the right place/profession, doing what you are passionate about? Yes_____ No_____

What changes do you need to make to implement the results you received? _____

_____

_____

_____

_____

_____

_____

_____

_____

_____

_____

_____

_____

_____

_____

_____

OVERVIEW/SUMMARY

All of the Course materials you have read and/or watched illustrate the power of The Law of Attraction.

Lesson 1   The Secret (Rhonda Byrne)
Lesson 2   E-Cubed (Pam Grout)
Lesson 3   The Science of Getting Rich (Wallace D. Wattles)
Lesson 4   Attract Money Now (Dr. Joe Vitale)
Lesson 5   Law of Attraction (Michael Loiser)
Lesson 6   The 11 Forgotten Laws (Bob Proctor)
Lesson 7   Down the Rabbit Hole (Optional)
Lesson 8   The Passion Test (Optional)

COURSE WRAP-UP ~~

Do you understand The Law of Attraction and believe it works? If so, how is it working for you now? _____

_____

_____

_____

_____

_____

_____

Which Lesson or Lessons did you like the most and why?

_____
_____
_____
_____
_____
_____
_____
_____

Which Lesson or Lessons did you like the least and why?

_____
_____
_____
_____
_____
_____
_____
_____

What is the most challenging part of The Law of Attraction
for you? _____

_____
_____
_____
_____
_____
_____
_____
_____

Can The Law of Attraction work for you? Why or why not?

_____

_____

_____

_____

_____

_____

_____

_____

_____

Will you share The Law of Attraction with others? _____

_____

_____

_____

_____

_____

_____

_____

What do you want for your future? What is your next step?

_____

_____

_____

_____

_____

_____

_____

_____

_____

♥ ♥ ♥ ♥ ♥ ♥ ♥ ♥ ♥ ♥

Remember! The Law of Attraction has been around since the beginning of time! It is a Law of the Universe! It is a vital part of our "being!" Believe in it! The Law of Attraction will work in your life **always**, and will touch the lives of everyone around you.

In Closing ~

Your beliefs become your **thoughts,**

Your thoughts become your **words,**

Your words become your **actions,**

Your actions become your **habits,**

Your habits become your **values,**

Your values become your **destiny.**

Mahatma Gandhi

We Are What We Think!

What We Think We Become!